BLACK

WHOLE

Jashua Sa-Ra

ACT KNOWLEDGING

I am eternally grateful for the divine making your presence known to me in my own person. You will all ways be my greatest teacher.

I thank you ancestors for having made spiritual science a culture to be innerstood and applied.

Thank you to my children for constantly infiring me.

Thank you to my mother for being an example of spiritual-centricity, continuous growth, and action.

There are many who have helped shaped me, from growing up in Dayton, to finding myself at Hampton, to coming into myself in South FL, to crystallizing myself in NY. I think of you all, and carry you on my journeys, safely secure in my smile.

To those who specifically helped me realize this book (knowingly or not): Angelina Stewart, Douglas Williams, Heru Ofori, Ian Jesse, Ingrid Desormes, Iusa Beckles, King Simon, Marcy Alexis, Nicole Acosta, Terri Merrideth, Community Word Project, Nicholas BK, and everyone who asked when I was going to do a book, I am grateful beyond the scope of the English language...this book is just a down payment for all that I owe my community.

LIVICATION

I offer this book as humble proof to my children, that the
universe is wet clay in our hands.
To the multitudes of seekers in the world, this work is a
loving notification that you are not alone in this.
It is my report to my fellow workers on the field that we are
winning.
I say to my ancestors: You are still here through me!

ORDER OF EVENTS

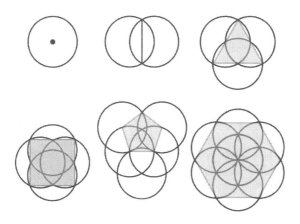

Poet's Note

Black Whole is a collection of observations on my journey as a Pan-Afrakan Spiritual Teknowledgist. I have a great love for my people, and an intense sensitivity to our condition. Freedom of spirit is something that far too many of us have not personally enjoyed to its fullest expression. I am a jali of Earthiopia. So the poetry that I share on stage and in print is my contribution to our healing and nourishing. We have many wounds to nurture. Many times we were back to back or side to side and have scars that connect like jigsaw puzzles. So we must remember to be patient and open with each other, and to acknowledge that our wounds are shared, not private property. Let us all have our own voice in telling our collective story. Here are the tears and smiles, the failures and victories, the challenges and innerstandings that I have acquired over the past few years. May they be of service to you in your journey. Love and Power

WHAT IT IS

it's the way the smile
stretches all the way
down to the feet
of home dancers
it's the bassline
in the key of
A Train accents
and swagger of southern ward
hips of palm tree sway
vernacular of corner store

it's the songs
that switch out of shoulder blades
when wings are illegal
it's the sports gladiators play
when warrior thoughts are lethal
we got the balls
to juggle worlds
with one hand
while power punching the sky

superheroes of simplicity
popularizers of poverty
it's the accidental trends we set
by maximizing whatever we get

it's the thunder
in our testimony
conducting our big bangs and baps
the compassion with which we make
heirlooms out of traps
we love us to death
we fear us to live

it's the rebellious sound of
confidence
when the odds
ordered silence
it's the faith
that fuels the effort
until the destinednation

it's the way language
likes to party in our mouth
and pose for nude poems
it's the way we look
in the sillhouettes
of babies' hands held

it's in the geometry
of spinning record breaking dance
b-boys to he-man
universe digitally mastered
gravity edited out
press playground
and make mockery
of modern physics

it's in the upper lip
and lower lumbar
it's the cathedrals
in back arch
the monument construction
of scalp grown crown

it's in the dual doorways
that dart away
from direct entry
eyelids the only protection
against casual specks
into souls that carry
instant revolutions
packaged and frozen

in practiced smiles
waiting for the microwave
of opportunity
to thaw out the future

it's in the uncomfortable smell
of hot flash freedom
that perfumes
our open wounds

it's how we lick salt
out of tear ducts
capable of oceans
and evaporate
into a higher power

it's the obvious god in us
that's what it is

Streets is wild
But my spirit safari

If you can't beat 'em
Call for backup

ALOE FOR ID

damaged skin
tends to grow back but
what
if healing is equal to
your depth perception
and beauty is the speed of
your acceptance

our curse words tender
with selfish
nobody to be mad at but
my selfness

the corners of our frown
bench press pain
upside down
without wavering we
strut in tiny mirrors
and make it big
as bad decisions
gone right

if there is a stairway to wisdom
it is a spiraling dominant gene
that nappy hair idolizes
there is only enough room
for everything

it's a mouthful of
mama's memory
teaching premonition
perfecting daydreams to
project emotions articulate
as new bein'
body language

parents don't need to get
their children back
get them forward
thinking

the creator is
the creation
creating
every thing
every right
now

SALVATION HAIKU

give it all to him
he washes away your sins
your toilet loves you

GRANDSUN

i sing the sun's song
from skies melanin blue
read from the chakra at south pole
for the snails with salt addictions
for the children
told to just say no
then handed a dollar
for ice cream f(tr)ucks
abstinence is the best protection
erections are just sponges
full of blood for suckers
with scriptures
written in red

i read the sign language
of def jams
that sound like a middle finger
to my forefathers
and the women
they would kill you for
easier for massa
when slaves fight each other
plus they make money
on the side bets

how deep goes the wound
screamed into our dna
we need an adhesive melody
a jazz band aid
damaged but we still duke it out
with bandaged armstrong
they play us backwards
but I still recognize our song
heavy with millennia
so the bass low from the trunk
of trees destined to be djun djuns
loud even if you ch ch ch cop us down

i the sound
when a ray bursts a cloud
filled heart
and in the lungs
inspiration is found
deep as time's pocket
riding a sex cymbal
elvin jonesin' till we crash
off the beaten path
paved by people
that raise babies in graves
rocked goodbuy on christmas treetops
dropped when the lie breaks
after they're caught in the box
lips glossed with masking tape
they can only hum their disapproval
rather than be responsible for truth
they refuse removal
of limitations

sky is the minimum
prerequisite
for imagination to mature
into immaculate conception
but we watch tv
without contraception
and get secularly transmitted diseases
from the same spin doctors
that offer you a shot of jesus
tryina take out shrapnel
with radioactive tweezers
we're all looking for the choir
that needs us
where our voice has a home
but you won't find harmony
until you know your tone
let the hyenas have their laugh
as long as you have your own

RAMEMBER

ramember
  when feeling nervous
  was rare
because no matter the situation
  community was there
  to support you
now if you make a mistake
the neighbors report you

ramember
  our elders use to guide us
  knowing life dangers
like the underground railroad
  hide us
  from that
  which would take away
  our humanity
such greedy traps
that hunger
for our destiny

ramember
  nourish your own future
  like trees planted
  over placentas
complacency plagues the people
  as a popular placebo
weapons aimed
against the holders

ramember
  once you get free
  put down the tools
  of slavery

ramember
  who you were
  before they made you
  theirs
ramember
  when land was traded
  for trinkets worthless
ramember
  when diseases were given
  on purpose
ramember
  they lied about it then
  and admitted it later
    once exposed
  and now it's different
  you suppose
from a rotted tree
only rotted fruit grows

ramember
  how to chart the stars
   how to hear the sun
    how to feel the earth
     how to find her acupressure points
     and do the dance
     of your greatness there

ramember
  how to look
  in the eyes
  of everyone you meet
    allies and adversaries
  and acknowledge god there

ramember

victory
is just
you being completely
you

Haiku Verdict

a coward still dreams
of a comf'table conscious
wake to sleep's cousin

HUNGERED

my crowded loneliness
is a buffet of fruitless texts
and intended calls
that stuff my tomorrow
until its ribs show

visits from beggars generous
with homeless egos
up for adoption
i can't afford my own
greedy i's

barely enough room
for another needy belief
my stomach so full
of two-timing truths

my slowed smile
takes bathroom brakes
i prefer to be alone
with my own shit

I Don't Believe You

i know god
like i know air
whether i see it or not
if you alive
i know it's in there
and around me everywhere
like water
that moves everything
from ocean to emotion
like earth that supports
the crawlers and the flyers
the ever present fires
in volcanos and hearts

same source
animated by same force
with a signature
on every art work
call it ugly if you will
beauty is in the eye
of the begetter
the care is in the
stitch of the sweater
i go to my creator direct
can't think of any way better

how can i be saved
through the efforts of another
i don't get strong
from the pushups of my brother
examples are made for following
stories are made for swallowing
because children are easy to ho out
i don't go out my way
to preach
but i do each one teach

and swing hard
on the demons in my reach

it's simple
the scripture says the body is a temple
so where else would you meet the most?
i tithe my blessings the way i gottem
through the people
priests and pastors
posin as ticketmasters
to a good life after
partying when it's showtime
let the manager
work out the details

i know god
like day and night
never fight about who came first
every couple knows
it's better together

i know god
like the healing
from grandma laps
the spirals in dna
and afro naps
like de ja vu
and thinking of someone
right before their call
comes thru

i believe in god
because i've known god
all along
and if you don't see it my way
i'm not gone say you wrong
we aint gotta sing the same song
for us to both know music
just show me your dance
or i don't believe you

REVOLUTION REEVALUATION

if a man is defined
by that for which he fights
what happens
when a man is stripped
of his home, his family
his pride, his god, his name
what is he then?
a reflection of his environment

nigger
made in the image
of its creator
lazy, ignorant, double life, adulterer
thief, murderer, rapist, addict, dead beat
so maybe it's actually
reniggers

i know it's impossible
playing against habitual cheaters
in a game they made
of course we feel played
their balls, their rules
we already know their moves
better than any other
it's all foul
with no free throws

only live once while you're young
then die daily till you're old
push paper until you fold
small enough to be hidden
as the remote
that gives us the control
absent in our lives
we work hard to find devices
for what we can do
ourselves

the unlucky break dancers
copped and locked
turned on our heads
until prison is a rites of passage
whether criminal or liberator
martyrdom is a career
whether thug or revolutionary
sex is an initiation
whether taken or given

how long
will we deify struggle
does the caterpillar
say
may the cocoon continue?
if they had xbox and nba
would butterflies ever break out?
patience beyond the point
of being proper
is asking for abuse
as if we had to
our lynchings have been
postcards in print
while we were
fighting for foreign freedom
overseas
bring the war skills home
but not to battle
with our own family

bruthas i hope this fit
into your ears
already cramped with the
amplified stereotypes
we've swallowed
feet first for the
breach of trust
misplaced
like tadpoles
with snake teachers

our children are changing
the world one trend at a time
but they are trapped
in exponential pimpin
impressed by the profiteers that
popularize our exploitation
the volume of our laughter
equals the depth
of emotional damage we dare
not liquidate

have the courage
to consider and care
for your woman
as intimately as your car
it's in the details
know your people's contribution
so you can measure your own

Hard work and struggle are not the same
One implies you are not up to the task

Manhood Haiku

why do you taunt me
with the ghost of freedom
responsibility

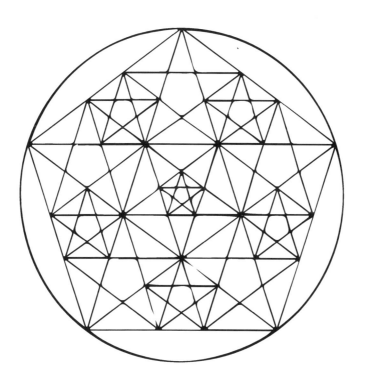

URBAN STROLL

three girls walk by
  smellin like cheetos & lip gloss
  waists move like stilettos
   in flip flops
  bodies sticky hot
   attitudes frozen from spine chills
   when boy men slobber them
    with illegal intentions
being cute shouldn't be dangerous

three boys board the 2 train
  lookin like all day sweat
   of boomboxed-in contortions
  learning early
   you must be acrobats
   to survive this damnasium
   of eyes that condemn them
   for adjusting to the darkness
when dancing becomes illegal
please notify
freedom's next of kin

a slice of watermelon on my plate
  aftertastin like pesticides
  texture perhaps permed
  colored like baby mice
   i still spit out imaginary seeds
   in protest of pretend produce
   with no future
or was that a religion i swallowed?

man snoring in the subway
  soundin like rotted chances
    and a truth full of cavities
  clothes stiff with yellowed pessismism
    dropped with coins into his lap
  kept lukewarm by the cold news
    he swaddles in
  avoided by frightened mirrors
    who walk by
    bags filled with on-sale escapes
    buy one get one flee
  his motivation has holes in it
    and long ago leaked his goals empty
he knows the sun
  won't be there in the morning
  and yet
he survives for a living

Mom and pop shop
  feelin like welcome home
    reunion with brothers and sisters
    from other mothers and misters
  smiles rub off on me
    like warm shea butter
  necessary discounts for old allies
    cuz gentrification raises rent
    like an undead army
      of franchises
  community traditions renamed
    neighborhood nuisances
      by newly hatched colonists
      who invade intellectual property
these four walls feel safe
but it's getting crowded with refugees

summer in the shitty

MEASURES

what is the measure of a man
who has outgrown his box?
but still lives in the factory
not delivered by another man's
save
can he find his own way out?
or will he be lost
in the looking?
alone stroll
among millions of
prepackaged souls
will he find some similar
to his height
and together will they fight
for the sunrays
if it has never warmed their sight?
or does the struggle make them
settle
for a bigger piece of cardboard?

when the acorn is planted
in a flower pot
why does it bother to grow?
does it know
it has already been cheated
out of its full potential?
and if so
is every miniature leaf
a reminder
that it's miserable?
and if no
does it daily pray
for the promised land
just out the window?
assuming the same

who instilled this
belittling behavior
will also surface as
savior

sounds like a long wait
for the wrong date
with the sundial tickin
i know we all wanna relate
but even people in jail
can get a strong mate
that's just not enough
when you know
the dealer is cheating
but you still gotta bluff
or you wanna pass
that piss test
but you still gotta puff
to take the mind
off this road that's rough
as unwanted sex
on unplanned trips
with your family waiting
for you below in the belly of slave ships
will your breasts still feel
familial
on husband and baby lips

i think it's better
to have eaten mango
and shitted
than to never have tasted at all
but love i think
is sweetest undigested
cuz even after it has rotted

in my bowels
i don't wanna let go
gripping my belly
and humming encouragement
to my constipated yesterdays
pretending these are labor pains
that will birth well lit tomorrows
longer than the life span
of recycled boxes
bright enough for acorns
to grow their own legs
enduring enough to travel
on another relation
ship
but for now
the highs and lows
are causing me
emotion sickness so
i will cling to this toilet
and wait for her
to pass through me

Have we given up on a happy life
And settled for a few
Happy hours
At a time
?

Excuse Me Missed

something's broken
as if sunshine missed the moon
you don't see me

and i innerstand how hard
it must be to look at me
i don't like zoos either
do the animals
think in their
captor's language i wonder

queen is no word to call you
who is holy water
in a motion temple

i need a tongue
that knows how to be simple
with the proper respect
for your rhythm
to have the conversations
exhausted ancestors sang for us
to light the way home

CLOSER

sometimes
people see me perform
and think i'm a good catch
i tell them
that's just photoshop
i'm too lonely
to be in a relationship

look closely
if you don't believe me
notice how the shadows
layered under my eyes
don't quite match
the smile
copied and pasted
from my past

come closer if you don't believe
let your nostrils fill
with the smoke
of my burned lovers
the choke of
i love you's
that never made it past the throat

you should listen closer
if you don't believe
hear heartache mocking me
making me its marionette
a fast talking dummy
using your laughter
to cover the obvious
this is just a show
i'm a fun
house mirror
broken
and seeing your reflection
in one of my shards
may amuse you
but your love is not superglue
don't try to fix me
hoping that when i'm good
i can fix you

kiss me if you don't believe
taste on my lips
dreams bitter
with abandonment
replaced by naïve wishes
that all i needed to be happy
was to make her happy
as if
i was her dreams
or she was mine
now you think
i might be yours

but what happens
when you wake up next
to a man emptied of aspiration?
how fast does your respect retreat
when you see me vulnerable
without a microphone?
will you despise me depressed
my laughter constipated with stress?
can you close your eyes content
in the arms of a man afraid
to be the power god gave him?

who will you be
if after years of
getting your goodies
i'm still emotionally unavailable?
how will you look at yourself
after I have had your best
and you've excused my worst
if you find i still
have feelings for her?
does it sound like i
should be committed
to a relationship
or a mental institution?

i'm too lonely to even fuck you
because i'd have to look in your eyes
share your breath
trace your neckline
adore you sweet
but you might like all that
and want it again
magicians do their trick once
so the illusion is not discovered
my emotional disappearing act
will not entertain you
i don't want to
have to explain to you
why it's not working out for me
so it's best that we
maintain our distant pleasantries
like each other's comments online
maybe hang out in groups
but don't fall for me

yeah you can come over
if you still don't believe me
let my constant jokes serve note
that i'm not serious about you
don't let my every day hospitality
fool you
into thinking you're special
because even though i know you are
i won't alleviate your insecurities
i'll let them dangle
from the well-earned compliments
i refuse to say out loud
because i don't want
your eyes smiling at me

how dare you think me sexy
did you not see my face
when my son passed
maybe you looked away
from my ugly divorce words
but i guarantee you
a grown man in
fetal position in a dark corner
aint cute

for now
i have eyes only for spirit
your titties don't impress me
unless they're in a babies mouth
your ass doesn't engage me
unless it's jumping to djembes
your admiration is uncomfortable
unless it's for god
your sex is not inviting
unless your bed is an altar
and you shout prayers
during orgasm

sistars
you gotta protect the gold
that springs from your heart
stop trying to nourish
thirsty deserts

i thank you
for acknowledging my light
but before i get
closer to you
i have to love
myself right

NIA

as beneficial as cars are
they can wreak havoc
pollution/accidents/5:00 traffic
so there are requirements
that must be met
before we let
somebody hit the gas

so how come
you don't need a class
a test to pass
or a current license
to get some ass?

even a relationship
isn't prerequisite
that's not good civil science
gotta get a study buddy
who wanna brainstorm
and build an ark
before getting cuddly

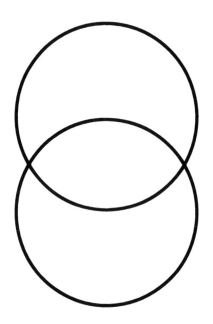

because babies
shouldn't be
experiments
nor bargaining chips
between estranged gamblers
when should a parent just
cash out

how long
can a man be whipped
before he lash out?
or cast doubt
into his own sea of thoughts

to avoid confronting
the actuality of being caught?

he must ignore
that he is a man
and thus ignorant
of his existence
he goes out
to give a girl the bizness
so catastrophe prone
are them
that hate their own

i used to wonder
how people could leave
their youts behind
but now i see
how it can be
healthier on the body and mind
to support a child
from a distance
if you crash every time
your lanes combine
but seeds' needs
are met locally
you can't mail sunshine

having a chef
during a famine
is worthless
so before your next trip
on the relation ship
already know
what's the purpose

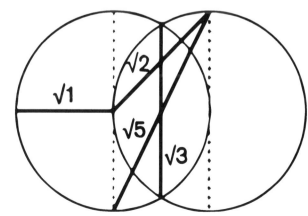

Next Wifetime

(to the one who got a way)

what childish humor fate has
to shove me towards
the shape of your spring clouds
and laugh when i autumn
mitt barren of a happy home
run by you

sometimes i wish i was blind
so i could stare at the summer sun
of your boldness
without seeming rude
and never lose sight
of your gold mettle yet
you dissolved in my blink

sometimes i wish i was deaf
so listening to myself
was not up for debate
no advisors' revised regret
no ambassadors' amicable ambiguity
only a pungent picture spoken
from the drumset that crashes
on the solo of my chest then
maybe you would sing
the hug i wrote for you

but my chances look like
makeup at a matriarch's funeral
ruined
application not worthy
of innerview
unqualified for photo albums
to be laughed at by siblings
we fashioned in your fathoms

i wait for the passing
of winter you gifted me
rapt in the dry ice
of your clavicle
hoping fate has made seasons
for second helpings
of first impressions

Tools for a Bedroom Garden

she said
"it's like paul mooney said
'a wet suppy
and a dry purse
don't add up'"
hadta hold
my gonads up
sleeveless
so i aint think
no tricks she had up

maybe it was just math
i was good at geometries
but this angle
wasn't 180 degrees
not even acute
thing to say

well i only make deposits
with long term investors
obviously
my interest in nation building
didn't impress her

she was a fly spider
but i couldn't calculate her
net and she sounded gross
so i rounded down
to a common nominator
she wanted the job
i had to blow her off
like eraser crumbs

i wanted sum
but i couldn't
count on my fingers
to persuade her

i wasn't trying to come
to an early conclusion
i usually divide the long way
meaning i take it slow
to avoid the confusion

but while i'm tryina see
if mirrors are lined up
she was checkin that my check
is signed up

i know women need security
and most call that
cash
but how we gone prosper
if our first purchase together
is yo a$$?

was i that throwed
thinking you had wife potential
when you was just a rental?

i guess liberty
aint such a lady

Scented spoils

i inhaled her
addictively
she is now
green and brown phlegm
trafficking my breath
carrying out
my disorders

her aftertaste permanent
mark her
unsavory words
my throat won't cough up

my lungs hold ransom
until i let go
but still
i haven't decided
spit or swallow

Black man
Do you have the heart
To take your woman back
From jesus?

WORK TO DO

we too often get mad
at the sister who
constantly encourages
because she sees us
strong
even though she's seen us
weakened
you mad at her
cuz she won't look at you
as a culmination of disadvantages
that's
a pity party
she just says get a job
cuz she don't have the words
to remind you
injured superheroes
still gotta get back up
to finish the story

she takes us into her nest
knowing our wings are clipped
and the role is flipped
so she goes out to get bread
expecting us to eventually get
spine up and again be the head
but when wings grow
ready for wind
yet we keep them tucked in
we can't be mad
if she asks us
to get a gig with groundbirds
but you can't sustain eagles
on chickenfeed
champion of the sky
is what she need
whether it's
yo girlfriend or momma

the upside down women
who grow men into babies
do us all a disservice
she should expect you to work!
it's not that women believe in the system
they believe in results
it's our job to show her
ours are better
the system survives on her
so for us to thrive in it
we'd have to become her
chapelle was right

if you don't want to work
for your historic adversary
then work for yourself
there are so many children
in your neighborhood
who could use a mentor
grow your own company
improve the home
that you live in
make it the palace
an empress deserves
the world
a child is made for
and then it's legitimate
to sit back and relax
our women have accepted rape
to prevent many of our
fathers' public murders
you can sweep the floor
before she gets home

regardless of the ugly
exchanged between us
who has had our back
better than a black woman?
don't let anybody lay
a finger on her

THE FAMILY'S PRAYER

our mother
which thou art heaven
hallowed be thine womb
life's waiting room

our father
who carries our thunder
supports the heavens
and protects those under

ponder the potential
if as a pastime
you and partner
posed in power positions
and perfected
pineal projection
or improved
belly breathing
according to midwife's directions

ummm question
if hospitals are for
the sick
does that make
a baby a disease?
does god really bless you
for a sneeze
if you got the mucous
from eating the cheese?

fda got us sick widdit
down on bended knees
throwing up
pleas
please please
sweet baby jeez

it's not only the truth
but also application
that give us us frees
and that mean
you gotta have technologies
children getting high
degrees
in the knowledge
of family trees
so they know
all the talents
at their dna disposal
and are prepared for the
generational curses
they gotta grow thru

keep their mind continental
but focus local
in libations to recollect
the correct genetic connect
to call collecting favor
for the future focals
but the vocals is old school
our family
whose art is creation
hallowed be thy work

Personnel Ad

dealer of refurbished hopes
seeks woman whose smile
sparkles in the dark
like big dipper lip gloss
on a face youthful with fearlessness

she will have eyes clear
as tubman directions
an honest laugh with
the potential to grandmother

facing harsh fakealities
she's able to speak hard lessons
soft as a cloud's breast milk

must possess a strong work ethnic
and keep an immaculate ma'at
for the company of gods

demonstrated ability to organize
dimples after disaster comes over
requires reliable transformation and
willingness to complete all optimisms

she has to always wear see-through
motives and walk runway flawless
in high ideals

she waits until I pull out
my lap before she sits
but knows to stand when
injustice enters the room

her hands should be small
enough to fit through the
electric fence around my heart
but big enough to protect
the weaknesses she finds there

she will recognize my long
silences as the hole i compost
my outdated loneliness in
and not sprinkle them with
synthetic words

she packs patience as parachutes
in case we fall in
lucky me
knowing i'm already committed
to a nationship

benefits include mental insurance and
members only access to private areas
compensation based on experience perspective
innerviews conducted on sight

SENSE ACTIVITY

my fingers are wanderers
in the serengeti
of her new growth

her cheekbones smile high
as god's college days
where i have studied the language
of her brows
and now i'm fluent
in their arch texture

bridged over two black
waterfalls of smiles
that god uses as windows
to let her light out
like exhales in slow mo
she takes my breath away

but she had he right
since the day
she looked at me
like a home movie
that our children could enjoy

the trace of her jawline
like merlot old vine
made strong to support
a full bodied mouth
that pulls two handed words
out of her sass

smile be watermelon sweet
while her fire speak
slices you in half
softly
as a serenade's last breath
and yet
i lay my lips againt those
shea-buttered pillows
that shape her syllables
and dream a motion scripture
starring her laughter
as my picture book of prayers
her neck is a rub and sniff hymnal
so i hum her collarbone
to ward off evil groupies

yes beautiful she be
but my eyes envy
my hands that rsvp
every time
her exposed skin invites
and they aint leaving the party
especially
if she turns off the lights

not until she drips
cayenne peach juice
not until her thighs burn
from the smile
stretched between them
not until the cat lady sings
another encore
and her knees are exhausted
from all the applauding
only then
i might take my hands off

but i'll hold onto her forever

TANKA

they say health is wealth
for community savings
getcha money up
misery is poverty
the work you do is the pay

OPEN POURS

her confidence is purple
walks too royal for blues
in pumps that up her
to hi level
by my measure
she is 45 kisses tall
laying down

my fingers have her memorized
but i need a calculator for her curves
her graphic seen best on
wide screen eyes
she has 3 dimensions of soft

her fragrance is prescription strength
still i get her over the counter
when no one is looking
we have not vowed insurance
so she helps me with the co-play

i wonder can i afford her
lavish life smile
she laughs in top shelf liquid
that comes easy
when i take her to eat out
i'll have another drink

against the day's head bored
her conversations are cushions
that never forget my shape
i could truth here all day

THE TIME I WAS YOU TOO

my atmosphere is sprinkled
with everyone's exhales
these lungs listen to
the whispers
songs cries curses laughs
that flavor forevery breath

i want to be undeniable yet
anonymous as gas passed
in the rush hour express train
take your breath away
have you considering
everyone around you
make you exhale slow
and find it hard to think
of anything else
let me write a
fresh air for you

have you ever watched
a star coaxed from
the throat of a flower
but not burned
by tight fit friction
a woman can stretch
beyond imagining
to let light squeeze
into this world
she is empressive

those moments are too
large for clock hugs

at what age do we determine
a person special?
for me it's on the first
mitosis
see the dream he
laughed so hard into her
that forever shook off
into a glow of constellation

watch how push and pull
made electricity slow down
into flesh already greedy
for tickles
longevity is found
in the instant, that
never ends

Haiku Surprise

We have a baby
I wasn't expecting but
She had it all planned

ENSURANCE

it wouldn't be so bad
to answer your child's
important question
with
"because i said so"
if you were also teaching
that you are god

doing something
that hurts your child
but you say it hurts you
more
doesn't sound like something
you should do
on purpose

curiosity killing cats
is good to know
when your town
is overrun by killer cats
but what does curiosity do
for little children

haven't you noticed
plants grow to the light
no matter how you turn them
but ashes don't blossom
no matter how you
burned them

i like when youts
have questions
because any occasion
can become a life lesson
a chance for lasting impression
so give them the best one
first and for most
moments afterward

i aint sayin
be perfect all the time
but they expect us to be
because that's all
god told them about you
i aint sayin
you owe your children
anything
cuz
i shouldn't have to
i'm sayin
don't show them
that you
fear/stress/hate
this place
show them the world
you dreamed of at their age
you used to call it
the future

CARRIED TREASURE

children is a word
  like love
    lost of meaning
the future does not
  fit into syllables
it is sized for
  cradled arms

fatherhood is itself
  an emotion
without which
  man becomes
    baby daddy
      spark donor

even without obligation
  i would all ways be there
    for the beauty of them
my self-singing songs
i stand as composer
  and applauding audience
memories melody made
  with my home grown
    improvisations

world tension seems small
  next to their dimples
natural muscle relaxants
  when i have a seat by
    the window to their souls
so fortunate are we
  who know what
    infinity hugs like

i wince when
  people call their own
   "kids"
  unless they really are
talking about young goats
sticks and stones
  hurt but
   in the beginning
    is the word

i just call them
  mine
because they are
  from the
   i n me
and we should be
  wise to call them all
    ours

parent
doesn't have enough
  vowel sounds
to carry the
  honor
   benefit
    magnitude
     responsibility
      treasure
of opening the door
  for the spirit

so if you done did it
  don't talk about it
be

LOVE OF LABOR

black
she deep as
space's love for time
after time
she modeled a home
shaped like sunshine
bending through melanin
richer gets the color of her laugh
i smiletan
nude as the truth birthing from her lips
too late to cover up

but i am not burned by her shining
magnetized
to grow right at her expectations
that i will reach the height
of mountains stretched out as earth awakes
alarming
how sugary sleep can sing to us
when we have childish tastes

i see the sea
well seasoned by tears
shaped like joy
falling from a flower between thighs
the straw that
life sucks souls through
into a fast splash of long choices

HE MADE ME BABA

his gaze is all rock no roll
steady as midwife hands
life holds his attention
like underwater breath

his eyes show hunger pains
for wishes carried on dandelion
that the world be clean
as the tears i laughed
at his crowning

his royalty is obvious
as the family he comes from
a face that announces
power has come to play

his hug is a reward
not given lightly
or without intent
specially prepared mix
for those with a taste
for integrity

his brilliance is super solar
above any spectrum of light
our eyes can reach
you need a pineal
to hear how he chews
constellations into consonants
behind a smile that's
a mathematical constant
i count on it
to solve any fear in me

i have faith
in his footsteps

Young brights
Eager to be tomorrows' noon
Are you for them
A cloud or a crystal

SON RISE

i approached as panhandler
for a recount of my pay
some days had to be missing

god must have been playing
miles davis too loud to hear
so the trumpet answered me
"soooo what?"

it refrained me
loud as a last breath
and yet i knew there had
to be another inhale
around somewhere

perhaps in a smile made
muddy with bodega wine
in a suicidal bra
exhausted from surgery/mix
in the cushions of a
fresh colostomy bag
i searched everywhere
in the greyhound parking lot
for spare life

she who was once his house
sent him a transfer
emptying her reserves
on his account
but he couldn't accept it
he just
withdrew

i hope he turned off
that damn song
when he got to heaven

ANOTHER SHOT

i love my people
enough to give my life
but my ancestors told me
it is no longer a time of martyrs
but of show-ers
so i stay live
with a handful of light seeds
i sprouted into speech
diggin deep
to cultivate the soul
when so inclined
pokin minds
at open mics
to plant question marks
from the exclamations
i bleed on these pads
period
in a cycle of moonsets
splashing out of pen
my mood is set
fairly settled
like rock paper scissors
but the social cuts
are too hard
to be wrapped up
so i show off
pus filled dysfunctions
like fresh greased tattoos
when i write bugle calls
for soldiers that snooze
for philosophers
on that booze
for the shackled family
that consider that ship
a cruise

you can't expect a cure
if you call a coma
a slight bruise
not all things
heal with time
some wounds
need attention and intention
comprehension of ascension
for when i get high
to escape low vibration
when what i really need
is internal elevation
activation of self save
but it don't fit in a microwave
and you can't wait
for commercial break
to find out who wins the last days
i grab a mirror every morning
and smile at the star
of my movie
the hero always has
to have a hard time
it helps humanize
our godliness
it doesn't hold us in check
it enhances our respect
for coming spiritually correct
and recognizing consequence
it makes us live
like the movie don't end
until we win
the bar don't close
till everybody gets chose
next round of victories
is on me

THE SOFT TRUTH

listen
to the scratch of pencils
positioning chromatic mode words
only saxophones can say
sheltered under cymbal showers
air brushed by autumn leaves
and indigo breezes
like butterfly sneezes
it's only loud to the attentive

listen
sometimes it's real quiet
but we always recognize it
like the light of the sun
or black of infinity

listen
it sounds like insides
of baby girl belly laughs
and afros dancing
to soft knuckle beats
braiding remembrance
thru sacred geometry
in secret sign language
of wombnipotence

listen
a soft slow gurgle
the pituitary response
to inhaling pheromones
from a collar bone
the sound right before a moan

listen
the hum of hot muscles
stretched too long
in smiles
made sticky
by sweet moments
that make men
love fatherhood

listen
to the rumble
of foreheads folding
over grandma's good eye
which is often too loud
for green eyes to hear
unless you

listen
to my favorite things
played by crickets
and lightning shows too far away
for ears to enjoy
i get tree ring tones
so i know when nature calls
collect myself
correct my health
direct my wealth
through wisdom
i can use some
and give some

listen
to YOUR TRUTH
and YOURS will lead you
to the Y in OURS

BREAK MY BONES

it's not like things were bad between us
she was just busy
makin it better
like the best go-begetters do
so i'm sure
there were other things on her mind
at that time

with balding buddhist boyfriend
in passenger seat
pipe tobacco breath
distinctly sickly sweet
chatterboxing champion
a word you can't get
in convos where it's no mo'
rengekyo
this hypocrite be cursin me
but for now
while mom is driving us
out of o state university
he provides the perfect distraction

me and big brother in the back seat
get it into action
corner of my eye
he's clickin in the seat belt
start wit sum'em simple
so he won't cry for help
knock his knee
sum'em low
so in the mirror
mom won't see

he
retaliate with a pinch on my thigh
equal invisibility
shoot
he saw through my trap
thought he would get dramatic
when re reacted
that's ok
i got other tactics
had nuff practice
getting on people's nerves

oh i got it:
i'm not touching you
"getcho finger out my face"
'getcho face out my finger'
his silent reply came quick
locked my pointer up
with a vulcan death grip

snatch back
and i'm like
'quit
witcho nutsack lip'
"intestine breath bastard"
'yo momma'
"yo daddy"
and just when he thought he had me
i dug deep
reached beyond my pre-teen thinking
and said sum'em
i must've overheard in my sleep

i was like
'mom dropped out of college
because of you
now we on welfare'
sat back confident in victory
look in my eye like
'so there!'

but his
1 year 11 month elder status
had him prepared
counter attack
delivered with precision exact
he came right back
like
"you was an accident"

all i had was an uncertain
'nu-uhhnn'
not yet knowing
what i was being acused of
but he was relentless
and had accomplished
to bring an accomplice
"mom wasn't josh an accident"

"yes"

it might be better for us
To use sticks and stones

GOAL DIGGER

her smile is lightning
massaged in molasses
it lingers
near dream edges
waiting for someone who needs night
to end right away
there is a pool of antique sunrises
in her dimples
and i for one am a collector
of fine heart
but she is no trophy for display
even though i fight hard
to win her everyday
she is tag team partner and play mate
she is survival workshop and play date
i check my reflection in her laughter
when people tell me
i look too serious
and can't see
how they expect me
to be
anything less
about her

To all my sisters
Who say natural hair
Isn't for everybody
Thas like saying
Feathers aren't for every bird

RSVP

hey beautiful
we should let our
powers combine
this is not a pick up line
this is an emergency call
i won't be bystander to the
heinous minds
committed against you
i know what you've endured

i know how you got
so much strength to fit
under one raised brow
and not be too heavy for
eyes to still roll freely
over any foolishness

i can hear it
in the late night ringtones
you know you shouldn't answer
again
and again
you do

i can count it
in your caution
to keep hopes
in a savings account
but you can't figure out
why you're losing interest
won't even give me credit
for checking on you
without a long term invest

i don't have to lift your dress
to know your kness
carry the bulk of your bruises
kneeling for gods too selfish
to notice you sucking
their prayers out
but religiously put
you down when they come
up short

i can taste it in the backwash
of a lonely drink
surrounded by smilers
that don't care how
forced yours is
as long as you're swallowing

i've noticed how quickly
your irises conceal the
weapon to which you fall
in love
you won't let another have
that power over you
and don't know how to
let yourself have it
so who gets it?
whoever you trust
to keep the lights
in

your eyes
proud ice cream cones
that refuse to melt in public
over greedy memories of licking
fingers sticky with your own liquid
we eat our shame without utensils
hunt for fresh company
willing to share suspicions

i can see it
in the ashes of your sons
powdered onto your cheeks
the ruin of your vulnerabilities
smudged pomegranate on your lips
the hesitation that
chalk lines your eyes when
men say and do
the right thing too much
your fingers tipped with
french guillotines to head off
any thought that you might be
open

it is i who wears your target as name tag
when something must be wrong
how many mistakes must i make
to be good enough for you?

it's unfair to prize a man
for how well he wins
at losing his culture
you can't have your mate
and defeat it too

i can smell it under
the perfume and body oils
lotions and creams
washes and sprays
gums and mints
you've been force fed
the myth of my death
as daily broth
your mourning
breath is
too upsetting to mistake

i'm alive
don't miss me
in my camouflage
angered species
must adapt to danger

beloved
your gain is dear to me
your pain is near to me
i invite you to visit my closet
i'll show you the x-rays
that say i shouldn't
be able to stand
the sight of another
significant other
worldly lover
insecurity cover
yet i see you

solution colored
and we dressed in matching
actions to easily identify
across the ages

look for the lion
who rejects the crown of wolves
to be the mane of his pride

expect him to succeed
every time
he opens his eyes
and he will sure as sun
rise
to the occasional
smile sparked by your faith

a sovereign emerging
to gather his beloved
you're invited to liveration
will you accept it?

GENETIC CURRICULA

i owe
an apology to my ancestors

for making complicated
these simple lessons

1. be honest with yourself
there are no oppressors
only people who force you
to make hard decisions

2. make the hard decisions
or they will be made for you
as sure as the sun goes down
whether you did anything with the light
or not
what is tomorrow
if no matter when you wake up
it's always today
what is later
if no matter where
the sun's shadow lay
the time is now

3. you can not run from what you fear
face fear like it's your bottom hoe
have fear
but don't do fear
have mind control over it
since it will not leave you
strut it in front of people
as if it's a game to you
and profit from giving comfort
or just release
to those in the streets where
our people are trapped

jerking off their bottled genies
rubbing erected egos
erupting in a wishstorm of revolution
they want to give a fuck
and don't as a desperate cry
for someone to show them
why they should

4. love like we get paid
a million dollars a day to do it
but only if done well
and our quota of inspiration is met
love like it's an ancestor invitation
to invest
with ten times the return
to bring it forward
and save enough community
to enjoy high human equity
on bonds of unity
love all people on the field
but go hard for your team

5. fight with invisible weapons
forged of vision
firm grip on handling biz
with cold steel determination
firing hot speeches
fully automatic liberation
loaded sound clips
powered by the people
of considerate actions
fight against abominations
in the eyes of babies
fight every inclination to be comfortable
with maybe
like freedom on layaway be
fight with the way things seem
if they do not match your dreams
because those are the gospel
of your dna

fight like your child's life depends on it
because it does
they deserve a today
worth waking up to

6.your children see you
and it is their desire
to in some way be you
but they do not want to hear
what you have to say
they who were already created
as the ultimate word speakable
by two inner voices
that sang in search of harmony
don't want us to
tell them what to do
they wanna see
what we look like
when we do it
happy stressed loving angry alive
so they can satiate
the demiurges they are
can you show them
the heaven you believe in
or just tell them to avoid the hell
they're conceived in?
raise gods
and gods shall walk the earth

7. it could be simple
as saying
know yourself
but thas not the full definition
of being free
you have to also be yourself
by choice
at all times
forever
amen
ra

BLACK

WHOLE

Jashua Sa-Ra

Made in the USA
Columbia, SC
14 April 2021